# Little Buddies
# PHONICS FUN

## Short Aa, Ee, Ii, Oo, and Uu

**Senior Editor:** Janet D. Sweet
**Design/Production:** Alicia Triche
**Art Director:** Moonhee Pak
**Managing Editor:** Stacey Faulkner

The mini stories featured in this book originally appeared in the *Itty Bitty Phonics Readers* series,
© 2002 Creative Teaching Press (developed by Sue Lewis, written by Rozanne Lanczak Williams).

# Table of Contents

**Little Buddies Short Vowel Sounds, Stories, and Activities**

The Sound of Short **Aa**

The Sound of Short **Ee**

The Sound of Short **Ii**

The Sound of Short **Oo**

The Sound of Short **Uu**

Review: The Sounds of Short **a**, **e**, **i**, **o**, and **u**

# Little Buddies Picture Clues & Phonics Fun Chart

Little Buddies like to have fun doing activities on their own—just like your own child—so look for these helpful picture clues in the activity directions.

 Write or trace or match

 Draw a circle around

 Cross out

 Say the name

 Color or draw a picture

 Cut out

 Glue

All of the Little Buddies characters in this workbook—Dan, Rex and Tex, Jill, Dot, and Bud—appear on collector's cards on the back side of the Little Buddies Phonics Fun Chart at the back of this book. Also included is a bonus collector's card featuring the group of Little Buddies and a review of all five short vowel letter sounds.

 **Aa**

 **Ee**

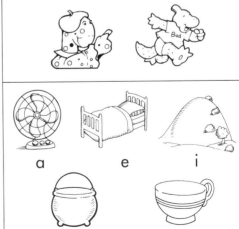

 **Ii**

 **Oo**

a    e    i

Look for the Little Buddies and their corresponding letter-sound pictures tucked into activities for each Little Buddies story. Have your child color, cut out, and glue the pictures to the inside

 **Uu**

o    u

of the chart to match with the characters on the back side. The Little Buddies Phonics Fun Chart can be used as a bookmark while your child enjoys the activities, or it can be cut apart to create personalized Little Buddies collector's cards—collect all 36 cards in the Little Buddies Phonics Fun series!

# Little Buddies Phonics Tips for BIG Reading Results

Phonics is one of the five essential steps that children must master in order to read. Practicing these five steps helps children learn to be good readers.

**1** **Phonemic awareness.** This is the ability to recognize that spoken words are made up of many different individual sounds. For example, young learners need to hear the beginning, middle, and ending sounds when someone says *cat*.

**2** **Phonics.** This is the ability to recognize that letters—and certain groups of letters—appearing in printed words represent different sounds. Children who have been taught phonics can accurately recognize familiar words automatically and can "decode," or figure out, new words.

**3** **Reading fluency.** This is the ability to quickly and accurately decode a passage of words for meaning. Readers who are weak in fluency read slowly, word by word, focusing on decoding words instead of automatically recognizing them and understanding what they mean.

**4** **Vocabulary development.** At this step, children actively build and expand their knowledge of the meanings and pronunciations of new words—both written and spoken.

**5** **Reading comprehension.** This is the step when children become purposeful, active readers by acquiring strategies to understand, remember, and communicate what has been read.

**Here are some tips for practicing phonics and promoting reading success at home.**

- Talk with your child all the time about subjects that he or she finds interesting.

- Sing songs, recite rhymes and poems with repeating phrases, tell riddles and knock-knock jokes, and share stories that you enjoyed as a child.

- Make up stories while traveling in the car. Start with a silly beginning sentence, such as "Once upon a time, there was a skunk in our bathtub." Take turns adding new sentences aloud.

- Have your child describe a favorite story character, family relative, birthday present, or costume.

- Notice and talk about road signs, menus, and advertisements with your child when traveling. When at the grocery store, have your child read the letters and words on boxes and cans.

- Keep a wide variety of books, newspapers, and children's magazines at home, and carry reading material with you whenever you have free time, such as while waiting at the doctor's office. Let your child see you read often for your own benefit so your child realizes that reading is important and enjoyable.

- Establish a reading time, such as after dinner or before bed, to help your child get into the habit of reading every day. Make reading time a warm, pleasant experience. Sit close to your child, snuggle, laugh, and have fun. As you read aloud, ask your child about the pictures in the story, the characters, and what he or she thinks will happen next. Read aloud with expression. Use different voices for the different characters and add sound effects to the story.

- Visit the library often with your child. Take advantage of library story times, and pick out books together to bring home.

# Meet the Little Buddies!

Each Little Buddy appears in a story that features the sound of a specific letter or cluster of letters. Meet the six Little Buddies and their featured letter sounds in this workbook:

**Dan** helps children learn the sound of short **Aa**.

Adding things together makes Dan a happy dinosaur! He can add ants, pants, hats, cats, and many other things that have the short a sound! Look for Dan in Little Buddies Phonics Fun Book 5, also.

**Rex and Tex** help children learn the sound of short **Ee**.

Rex and Tex are enthusiastic and energetic dinosaur twins! They like the letter e—especially its short vowel sound in the middle of their names. Look for Rex and Tex in Little Buddies Phonics Fun Book 5, also.

**Jill** helps children learn the sound of short **Ii**.

Jill may be a little dinosaur, but she is incredibly impressive when she hits baseballs, kicks soccer balls, and swims! Look for Jill in Little Buddies Phonics Fun Book 5, also.

**Dot** helps children learn the sound of short **Oo**.

Once you meet Dot, it's easy to understand that she is obviously fond of spots! This polka-dotted dinosaur often wears clothes with dots and spots. Even her drawings have dots and spots! Look for Dot in Little Buddies Phonics Fun Book 5, also.

**Bud** helps children learn the sound of short **Uu**.

Bud is a fun-loving dinosaur who likes to run and jump in mud! Of course, that means he'll end up in the tub. Look for Bud in Little Buddies Phonics Fun Book 5, also.

Each Little Buddies Phonics Fun story features words that target a specific short vowel sound. Parents, prior to reading each story, you may want to read these words aloud with your child. Emphasizing short vowel sounds and their corresponding letters helps support your child's mastery of phonics, a critical early step in achieving reading success.

The story **Dan Can Add** features these words with the sound of short **a**:

- Dan
- can
- add
- ants
- pants
- hats
- cats
- bags
- and
- tags
- pans
- fans
- can't

The story **Rex and Tex Out West** features these words with the sound of short **e**:

- Rex
- Tex
- west
- went
- set
- tent
- rest
- felt
- wet
- let
- them
- fed
- sent
- bed
- end

The story **Little Miss Jill** features these words with the sound of short **i**:

- will
- hit
- Little
- Miss
- Jill
- will
- kick
- it
- in
- swim
- win
- this

The story **Dot's Spots** features these words with the sound of short **o**:

- Dot
- spots
- lots
- Dot's
- spot
- dog
- frog
- log
- on
- hot
- hop

The story **Bud in the Mud** features these words with the sound of short **u**:

- Bud
- up
- run
- Jump
- mud
- thud
- Sun
- fun
- tub
- rub-a-dub-dub
- suds
- Bubbles
- plug
- hug

The story **Dan and Dot** features these words that review the sounds of short **a**, **e**, **i**, **o**, and **u**:

- Dan
- and
- Dot
- spot
- bag
- hat
- in
- cat
- pants
- on
- spots
- rat
- hops
- runs
- after
- run
- Then
- stop
- nap

# Dan Can Add

 Trace the letter **Aa**.

These things have the sound of short **a**, as in **fan**.

 Color the fan.

 Cut out the fan.

 Glue it on the short **Aa** space inside
the Little Buddies Phonics Chart.

# Aa

Circle each letter **a**.

a      c      d      a

c      a      a      d

Circle each letter **A**.

V      A      A      N

A      N      V      A

Circle the things that have the short **a** sound, as in **fan**.

Little Buddies Phonics Fun • Book 4 • Gr. PreK–K © 2012 Creative Teaching Press

Dan can add ants.

 Trace the letter **A** in Andy.

 Trace the letter **a** in can.

Dan can add pants.

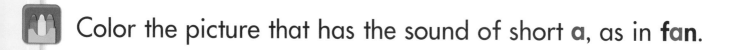

Color the picture that has the sound of short **a**, as in **fan**.

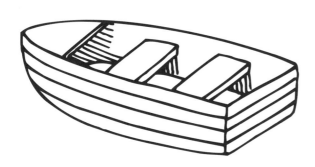

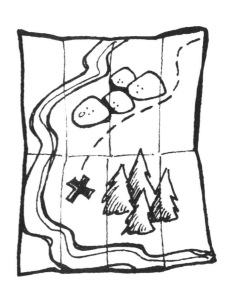

Little Buddies Phonics Fun • Book 4 • Gr. PreK–K © 2012 Creative Teaching Press

Dan can add hats.

 Circle the things that have the sound of short **a**, as in **fan**.

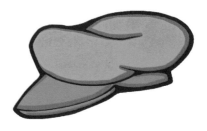

Dan can add cats.

Circle the things that have the sound of short **a**.

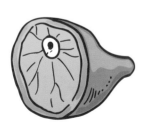

Little Buddies Phonics Fun • Book 4 • Gr. PreK–K © 2012 Creative Teaching Press

Dan can add bags
and tags.

 Cross out the things that do **not** have the sound
of short **a**.

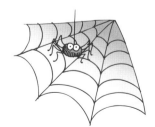

Little Buddies Phonics Fun • Book 4 • Gr. PreK–K © 2012 Creative Teaching Press

Dan can add pans.

 Draw pictures of 2 things that have the sound of short **a**.

Little Buddies Phonics Fun • Book 4 • Gr. PreK–K © 2012 Creative Teaching Press

Dan can add fans.

 Match each picture to its story word.

  •  •  pants

  •  •  fans

  •  •  Dan

But Dan can't add cookies!

 Write the missing letter.

   ___nts

   f___ns

Little Buddies Phonics Fun • Book 4 • Gr. PreK–K © 2012 Creative Teaching Press

# "I Can!" Mini Book

**Mini Book Directions**: Tear out pages 17–20. Cut the pages apart along the solid lines. Arrange the pages together in order. Staple the pages to make a little book that begins with **I Can**! Enjoy your book!

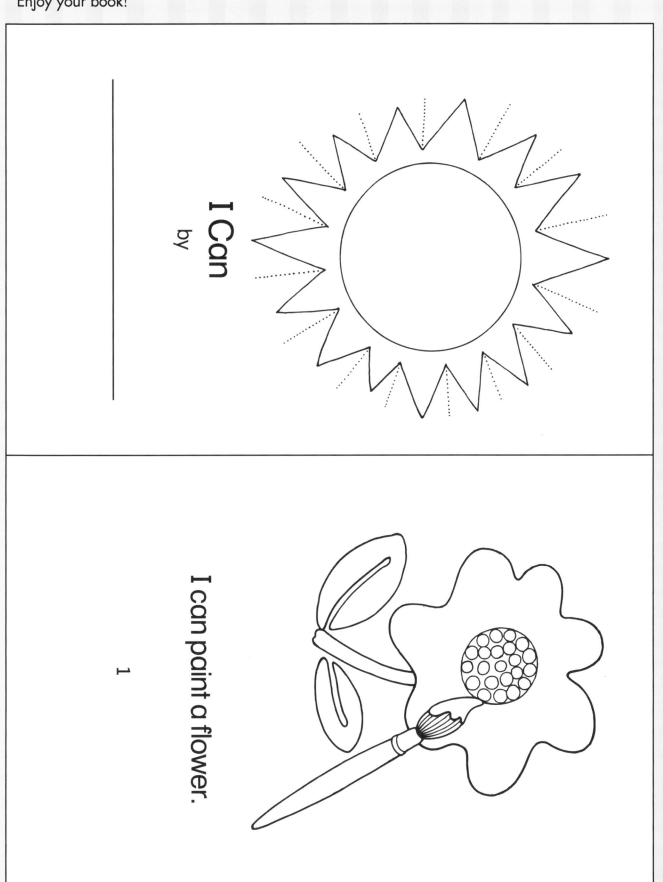

I Can
by

I can paint a flower.

1

Little Buddies Phonics Fun • Book 4 • Gr. PreK–K © 2012 Creative Teaching Press

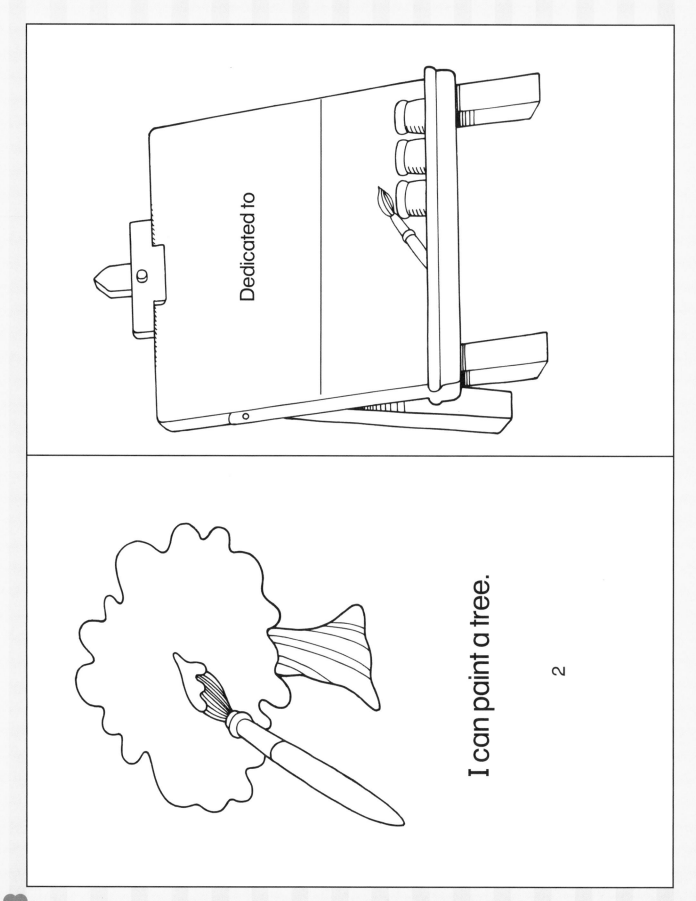

Dedicated to

I can paint a tree.

2

I can paint a picture.

5

I can paint the sun.

3

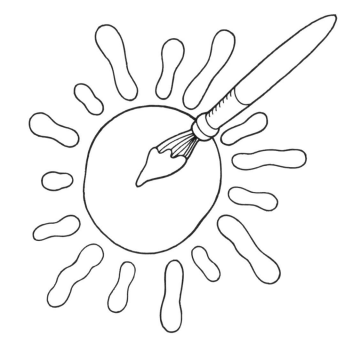

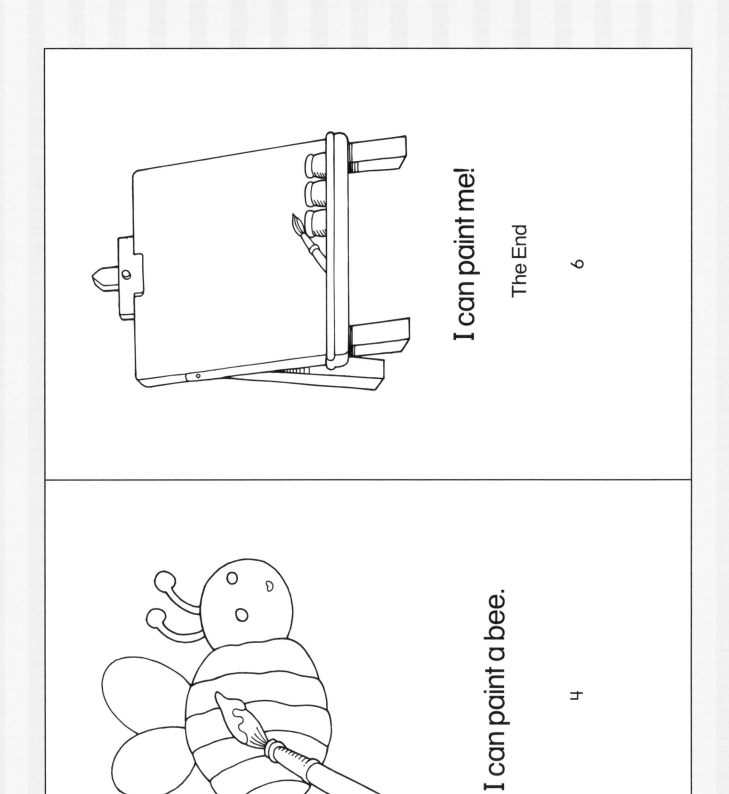

I can paint me!

The End

6

I can paint a bee.

4

# Rex and Tex Out West

 Trace the letter **Ee**.

These things have the sound of short **e**, as in **bed**.

 Color the bed.

 Cut out the bed.

 Glue it on the short **Ee** space inside the Little Buddies Phonics Chart.

Little Buddies Phonics Fun • Book 4 • Gr. PreK–K © 2012 Creative Teaching Press

# Ee

Circle each letter **e**.

e     a     c     e

c     e     a     e

Circle each letter **E**.

E     E     F     E

F     E     E     F

Circle the things that have the sound of short **e**, as in **bed**.

Rex and Tex packed up
to go west.

Trace the letter **E** in ___Ella___.

Trace the letter **e** in ___west___.

Off they went!

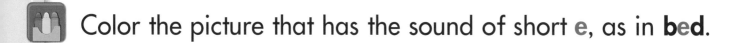

Color the picture that has the sound of short **e**, as in **bed**.

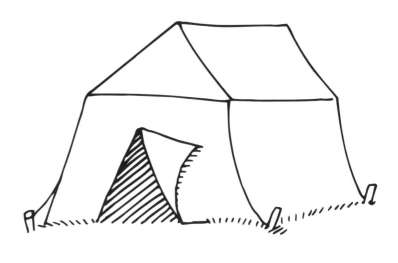

They set up a tent.

 Circle the things that have the sound of short **e**, as in **bed**.

Little Buddies Phonics Fun • Book 4 • Gr. PreK–K © 2012 Creative Teaching Press

Rex and Tex went to rest
in the tent.

 Cross out the things that do **not** have the sound of short **e**.

Little Buddies Phonics Fun • Book 4 • Gr. PreK–K © 2012 Creative Teaching Press

Rex and Tex felt all wet!

 Match each picture to its story word.

    •                    •  tent

    •                    •  rest

    •                    •  wet

They went to Mom.
She let them in.

 Draw pictures of 2 things that have the sound of short e.

Mom fed them and
sent them to bed.

 Cross out the story words that do **not** have the letter **e**.

Rex      west      wet

fed      off      rest

tent      and      bed

The End!

 Say the name of each picture.

 Match each picture to its letter sound.

 •        • **short e** •

 •        • **short a** •

# "Spring Eggs" Mini Book

**Mini Book Directions**: Tear out pages 31–34. Cut the pages apart along the solid lines. Arrange the pages together in order. Staple the pages to make a little book that begins with **Spring Eggs**. Enjoy your book!

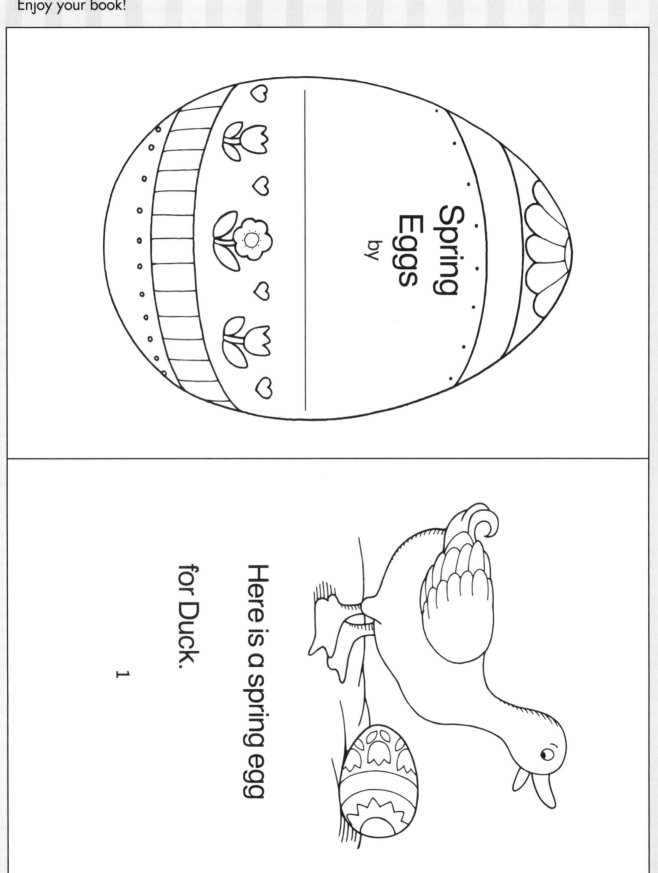

Spring Eggs
by

Here is a spring egg for Duck.

1

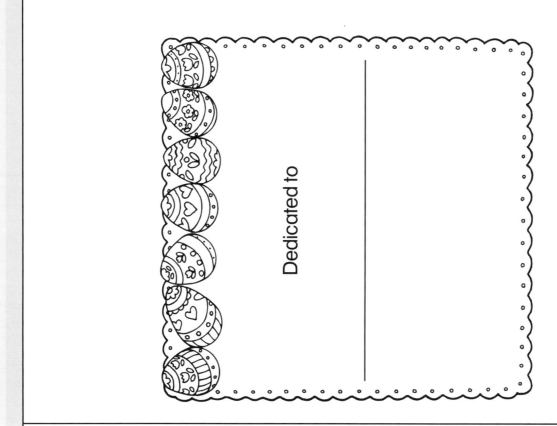

Dedicated to

_____

Here is a spring egg

for Hen.

2

Here is a spring egg

for you.

5

Here is a spring egg

for Turtle.

3

And here is one for you

to make!

The End

6

Here is a spring egg

for Snake.

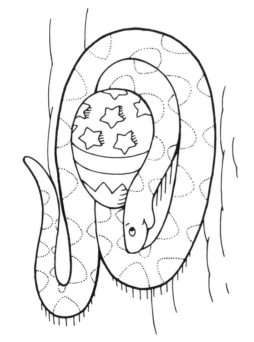

4

Little Buddies Phonics Fun • Book 4 • Gr. PreK–K © 2012 Creative Teaching Press

# Little Miss Jill

 Trace the letter **Ii**.

These things have the sound of short **i**, as in **hill**.

 Color the hill.

 Cut out the hill.

 Glue it on the short **Ii** space inside the Little Buddies Phonics Chart.

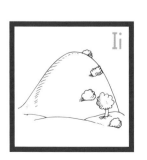

# Ii

Circle each letter i.

i    j    i    j

l    j    l    i

Circle each letter I.

T    I    L    I

I    L    J    I

Circle the things that have the sound of short **i**, as in **hill**.

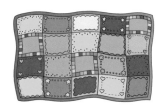

Who will hit the ball?

 Trace the letter I in  Indiana.

 Trace the letter i in 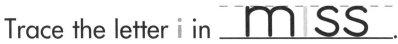 miss.

Little Buddies Phonics Fun • Book 4 • Gr. PreK–K © 2012 Creative Teaching Press

Little Miss Jill will!

 Color the picture that has the sound of short i, as in **hill**.

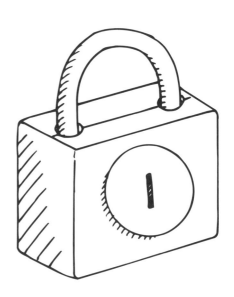

Who will kick it in the net?

 Circle the things that have the sound of short i, as in **hill**.

Little Miss Jill will!

 Match each picture to its story word.

hit

Jill

kick

Little Buddies Phonics Fun • Book 4 • Gr. PreK–K © 2012 Creative Teaching Press

Who will swim
and win the race?

 Cross out the things that do **not** have the sound of short **i**.

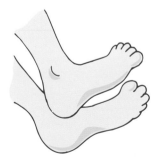

Little Buddies Phonics Fun • Book 4 • Gr. PreK–K © 2012 Creative Teaching Press

Little Miss Jill will!

 Say the name of each picture.

 Match each picture to its letter sound.

 • • **short i** •

 • • **short e** •

*Little Buddies Phonics Fun • Book 4 • Gr. PreK–K © 2012 Creative Teaching Press*

Who will win this?

**X** Cross out the words that do **not** have the letter **i**.

| | | |
|---|---|---|
| Miss | will | Jill |
| swim | who | in |
| ball | net | team |

We all will!

 Cut out the letters in the boxes below.

 Glue each letter next to a picture with that short vowel sound.

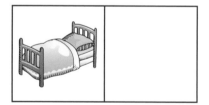

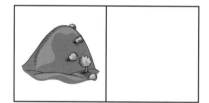

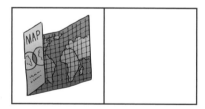

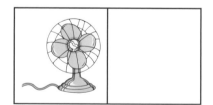

| a | e | i | a | e | i |

Little Buddies Phonics Fun • Book 4 • Gr. PreK–K © 2012 Creative Teaching Press

# "In Went" Mini Book

**Mini Book Directions:** Tear out pages 45–48. Cut the pages apart along the solid lines. Arrange the pages together in order. Staple the pages to make a little book that begins with **In Went**. Enjoy your book!

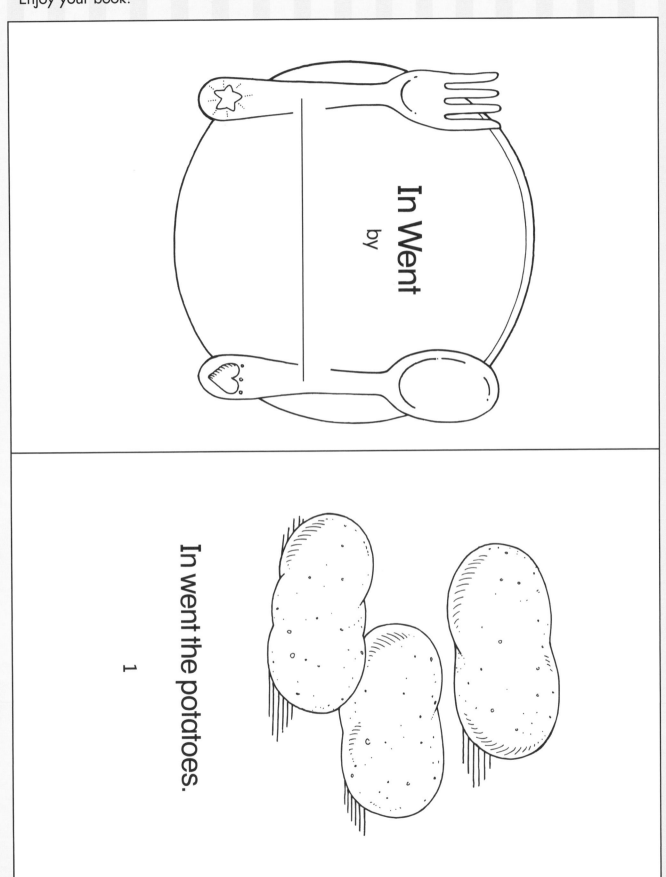

In Went
by

In went the potatoes.

1

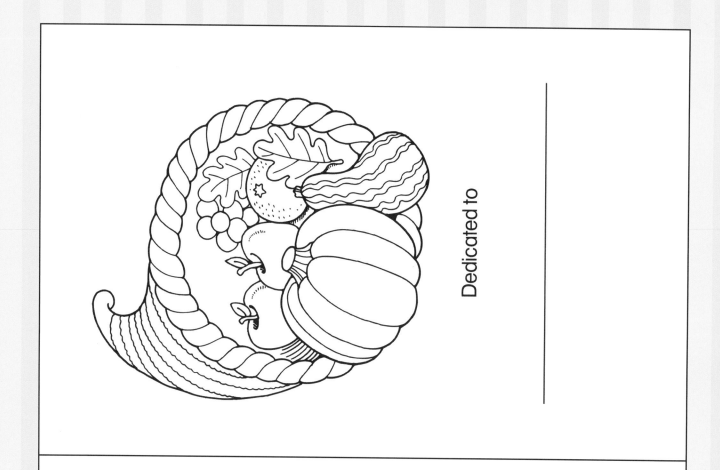

Dedicated to

_____

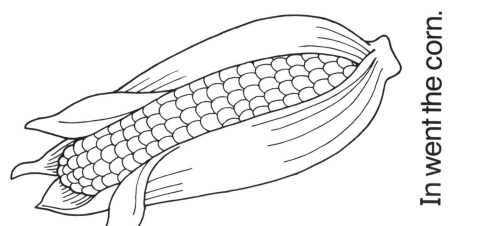

In went the corn.

2

In went the rolls.

5

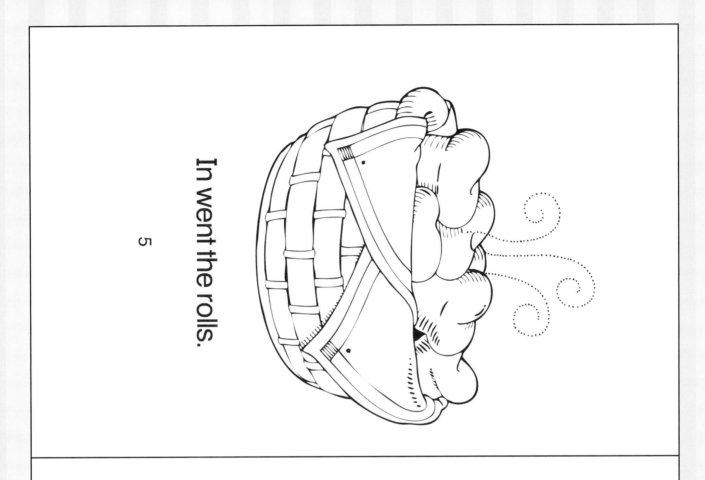

In went the turkey.

3

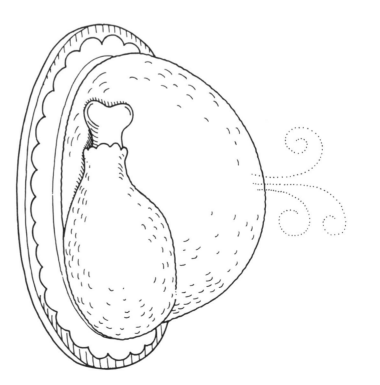

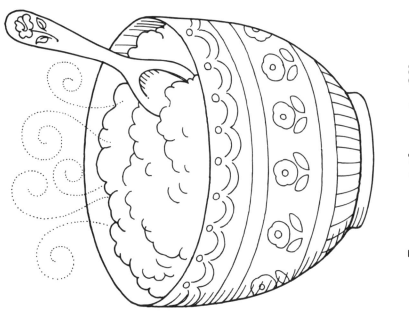

Now I am full!

The End

6

In went the stuffing.

4

# Dot's Spots

 Trace the letter **Oo**.

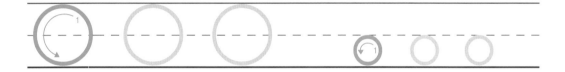

These things have the sound of short **o**, as in **pot**.

 Color the pot.

 Cut out the pot.

 Glue it on the short **Oo** space inside the Little Buddies Phonics Chart.

Little Buddies Phonics Fun • Book 4 • Gr. PreK–K © 2012 Creative Teaching Press

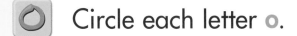

#  Oo

 Circle each letter o.

o      o      a      e

e      o      a      o

 Circle each letter O.

O      Q      O      C

Q      C      O      Q

 Circle the things that have the sound of short o, as in **pot**.

Little Buddies Phonics Fun • Book 4 • Gr. PreK–K © 2012 Creative Teaching Press

Dot loves spots.

 Trace the letter o in Olivia.

 Trace the letter o in spot.

She draws lots of spots.

 Color the picture that has the sound of short **o**, as in **p**o**t**.

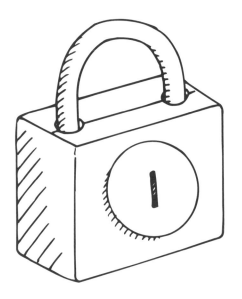

Dot's spot is a dog.

 Circle the things that have the sound of short o, as in p**o**t.

Dot's spot is a frog.

 Cross out the things that do **not** have the sound of short **o**.

Little Buddies Phonics Fun • Book 4 • Gr. PreK–K © 2012 Creative Teaching Press

Dot's spot is a log.

 Draw pictures of 2 things that have the sound of short o.

The frog is on the log.

 Match each picture to its story word.

 •                    • **frog**

 •                    • **dog**

 •                    • **log**

Little Buddies Phonics Fun • Book 4 • Gr. PreK–K © 2012 Creative Teaching Press

Dot's spot is hot!

 Cross out the words that do **not** have the letter **o**.

| | | |
|---|---|---|
| dog | spot | hop |
| can | draws | hot |
| frog | lots | she |

Little Buddies Phonics Fun • Book 4 • Gr. PreK–K © 2012 Creative Teaching Press

Dot's spots can hop,
hop, hop!

 Write the missing letter.

h __ p

h __ t

# "Jump, Frog!" Mini Book

**Mini Book Directions**: Tear out pages 59–62. Cut the pages apart along the solid lines. Arrange the pages together in order. Staple the pages to make a little book that begins with **Jump, Frog!** Enjoy your book!

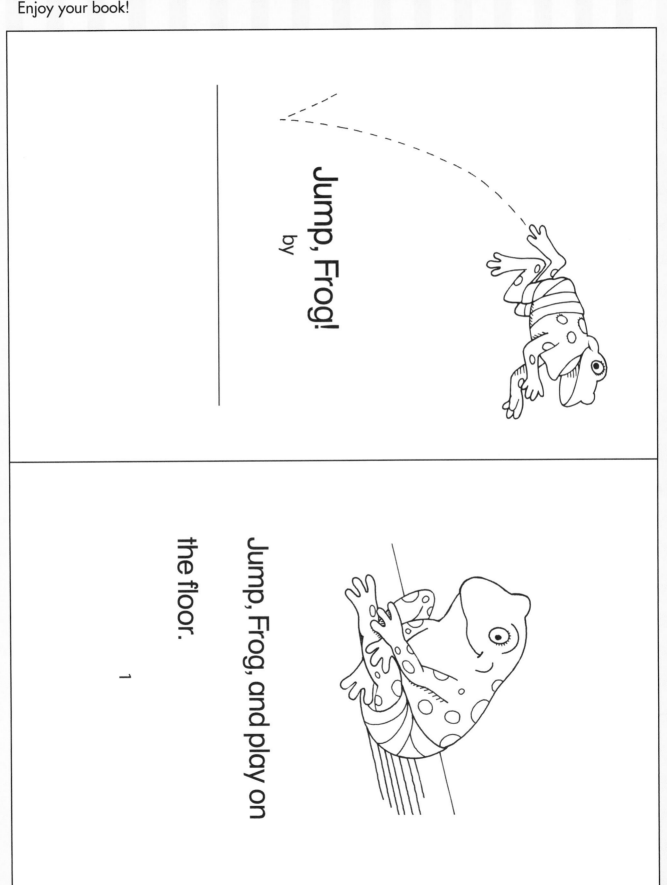

Jump, Frog!
by

Jump, Frog, and play on the floor.

1

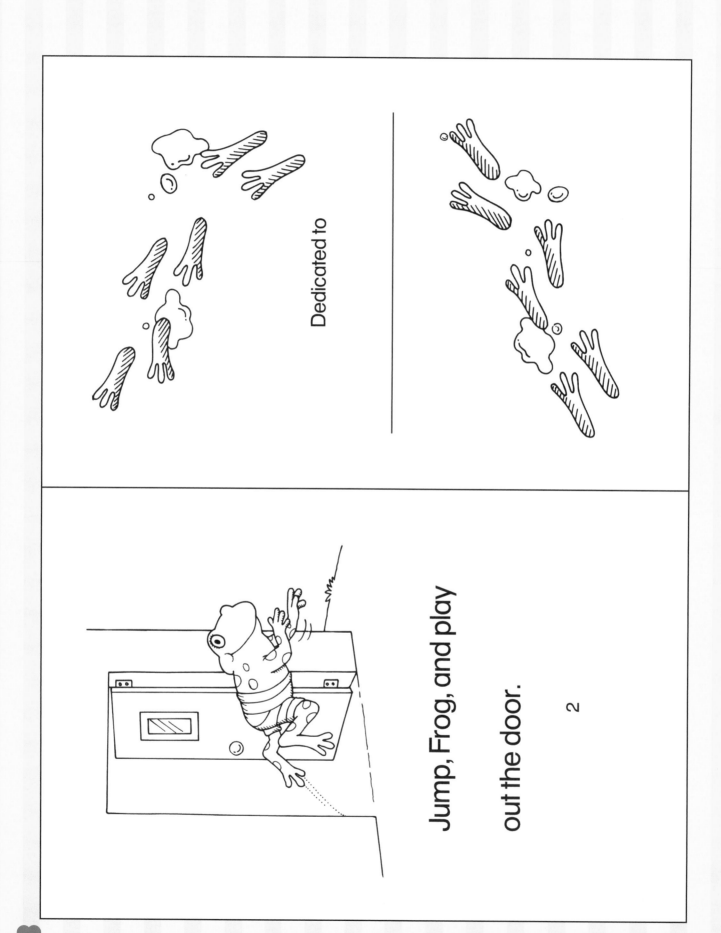

Dedicated to

Jump, Frog, and play

out the door.

2

Jump, Frog, and play
by the tree.

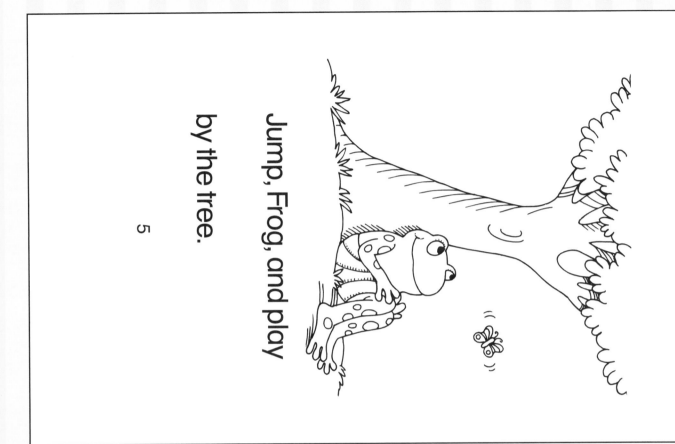

5

Jump, Frog, and play
on the rocks.

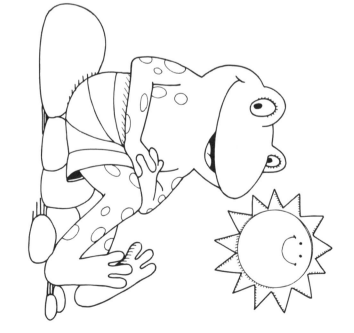

3

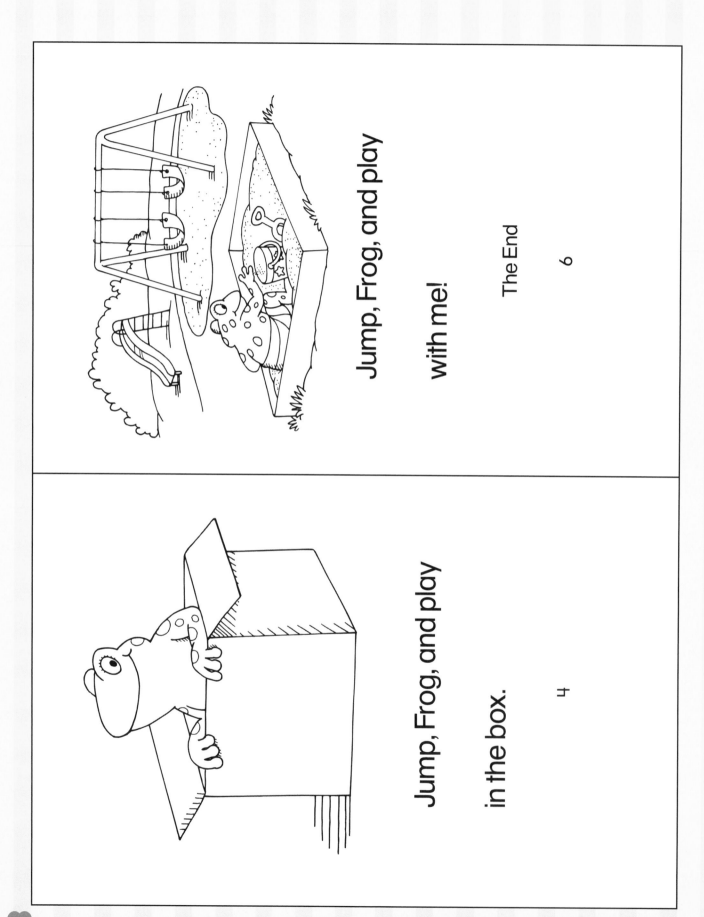

Jump, Frog, and play

with me!

The End

6

Jump, Frog, and play

in the box.

4

Little Buddies Phonics Fun • Book 4 • Gr. PreK–K © 2012 Creative Teaching Press

# Bud in the Mud

 Trace the letter **Uu**.

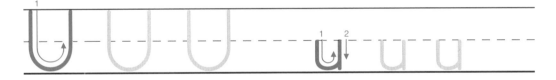

These things have the sound of short **u**, as in **cup**.

        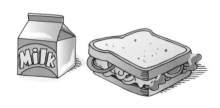

 Color the cup.

 Cut out the cup.

 Glue it on the short **Uu** space inside the Little Buddies Phonics Chart.

# Uu

Circle each letter **u**.

a     u     n     u

u     o     n     u

Circle each letter **U**.

U     A     J     U

N     U     O     J

Circle the things that have the sound of short **u**, as in **cup**.

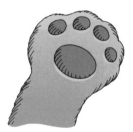

Little Buddies Phonics Fun • Book 4 • Gr. PreK–K © 2012 Creative Teaching Press

Bud gets up.

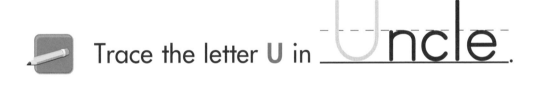

Trace the letter **U** in _Uncle_.

Trace the letter **u** in _mud_.

Run, run, run!

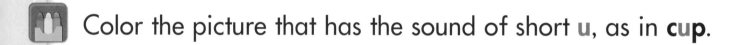 Color the picture that has the sound of short **u**, as in **cup**.

Jump in the mud
with a thud, thud, thud!

 Circle the things that have the sound of short **u**,
as in **cup**.

Sun on the mud is fun
for Bud.

 Match each picture to its story word.

    •       • **run**

    •       • **sun**

    •       • **mud**

Go up to the tub with the
mud on Bud.

 Cross out the things that do **not** have the sound of
short **u**.

Little Buddies Phonics Fun • Book 4 • Gr. PreK–K © 2012 Creative Teaching Press

Bubbles and suds with
a rub-a-dub-dub!

 Say the name of each picture.

Match each picture to its letter sound.

 • • **short u** • •

 • • **short o** • •

All clean now, so pull the plug.

 Circle the words that have the letter **u**.

| | | |
|---|---|---|
| mud | thud | now |
| fun | with | jump |
| glug | into | run |

Now it's time for a
hug, hug, hug!

 Write the missing letter.

t ___ b

pl ___ g

# "Bugs" Mini Book

**Mini Book Directions**: Tear out pages 73–76. Cut the pages apart along the solid lines. Arrange the pages together in order. Staple the pages to make a little book that begins with **Bugs**. Enjoy your book!

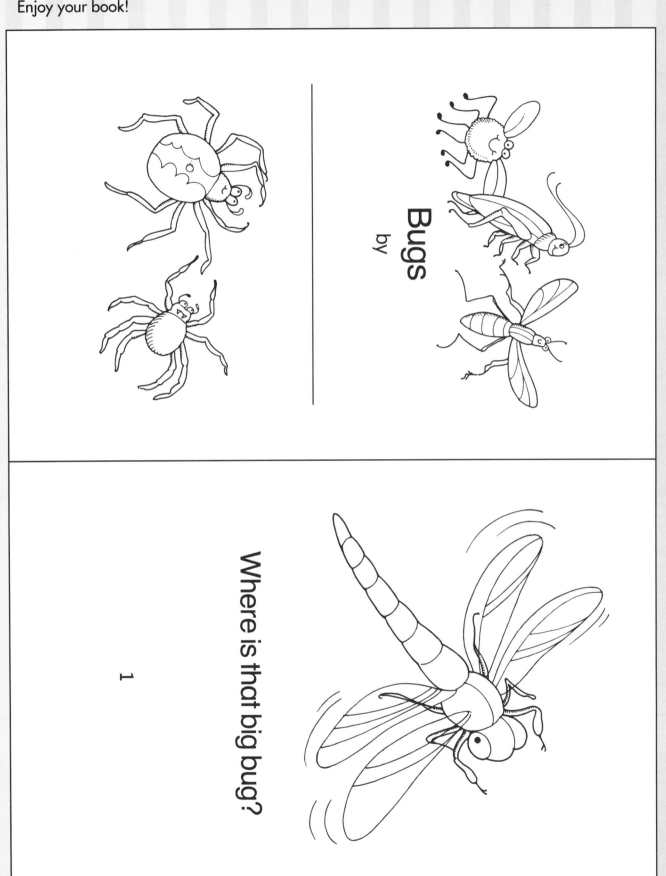

Bugs
by

Where is that big bug?

1

Little Buddies Phonics Fun • Book 4 • Gr. PreK–K © 2012 Creative Teaching Press

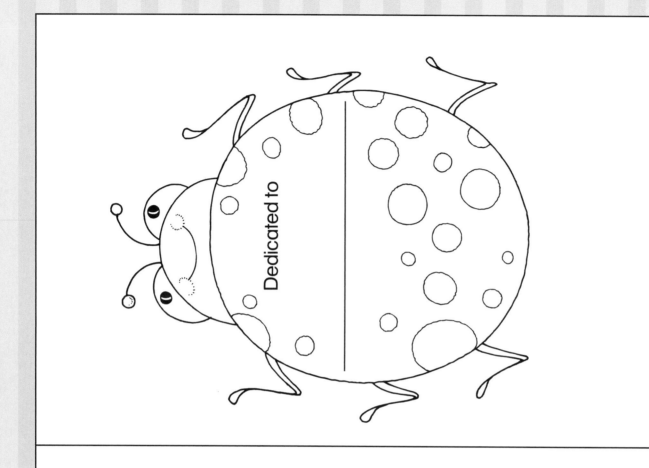

Dedicated to

Where is that little bug?

2

Little Buddies Phonics Fun • Book 4 • Gr. PreK–K © 2012 Creative Teaching Press

Where is that
pesky bug?

5

Where is that
mean bug?

3

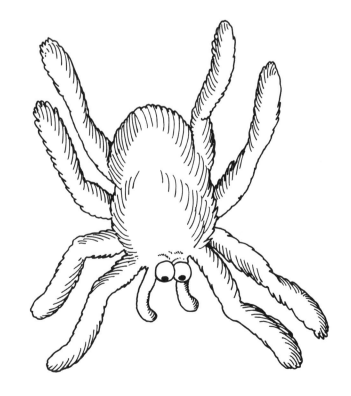

Little Buddies Phonics Fun • Book 4 • Gr. PreK–K © 2012 Creative Teaching Press

There it is. Swat!

The End

6

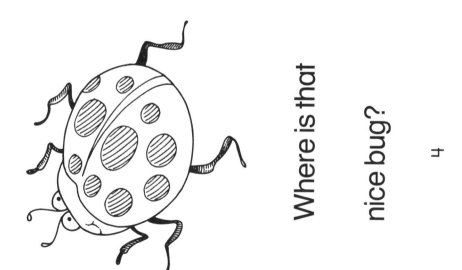

Where is that
nice bug?

4

Little Buddies Phonics Fun • Book 4 • Gr. PreK–K © 2012 Creative Teaching Press

# Dan and Dot

 Trace the letters **A, E, I, O, U**.

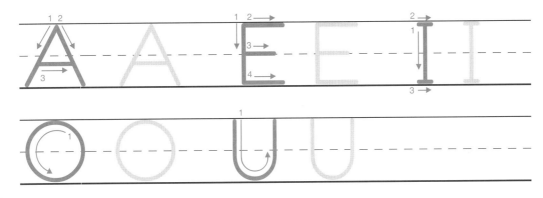

 Trace the letters **a, e, i, o, u**.

 Color the picture.

 Cut out the picture.

 Glue it on the short **a-e-i-o-u**
space inside the Little Buddies Phonics Chart.

Match the letters
**a**, **e**, **i**, **o**, and **u**.

a  •                    •  o

e  •                    •  u

i  •                    •  a

o  •                    •  e

u  •                    •  i

 Match the letters
**A**, **E**, **I**, **O**, and **U**.

U  •                    •  E

E  •                    •  O

I  •                    •  A

O  •                    •  U

A  •                    •  I

*Little Buddies Phonics Fun • Book 4 • Gr. PreK–K © 2012 Creative Teaching Press*

Dan and Dot spot a bag...

 Circle the things that have the sound of short **a**, as in **f**a**n**, or short **o**, as in **p**o**t**.

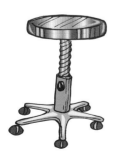

... and a hat in the bag...

Circle the things that have the sound of short **e**, as in **bed**.

Little Buddies Phonics Fun • Book 4 • Gr. PreK–K © 2012 Creative Teaching Press

... and a cat in the hat...

 Color the picture that has the sound of short **i**, as in **hill**.

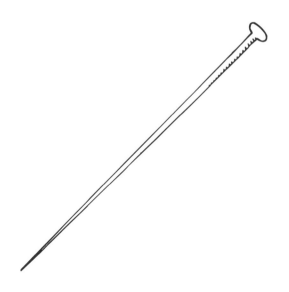

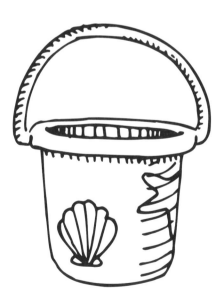

... and pants on the cat.

 Circle the things that have the sound of short **u**, as in **cup**.

The cat in the hat
spots a rat!

 Match the pictures that have the short **a** and
short **o** sounds.

The cat runs after the rat.

 Match the pictures that have short **o** and short **u** sounds.

Dan and Dot run after the cat.

 Say the name of each word.

Match each story word to its letter sound.

rat • • short a • • hops

spot • • short o • • pants

Little Buddies Phonics Fun • Book 4 • Gr. PreK–K © 2012 Creative Teaching Press

Then they all stop for a nap.

 Cut out the letters in the boxes below.

 Glue each letter next to a picture with that short vowel sound.

      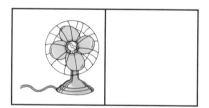

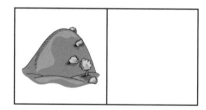   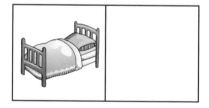

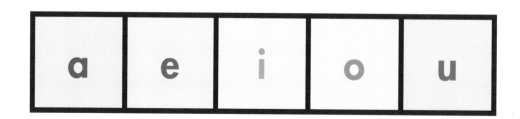

a   e   i   o   u

Little Buddies Phonics Fun • Book 4 • Gr. PreK–K © 2012 Creative Teaching Press

# "Can You Tell?" Mini Book

**Mini Book Directions**: Tear out pages 87–90. Cut the pages apart along the solid lines. Arrange the pages together in order. Staple the pages to make a little book that begins with **Can You Tell?** Enjoy your book!

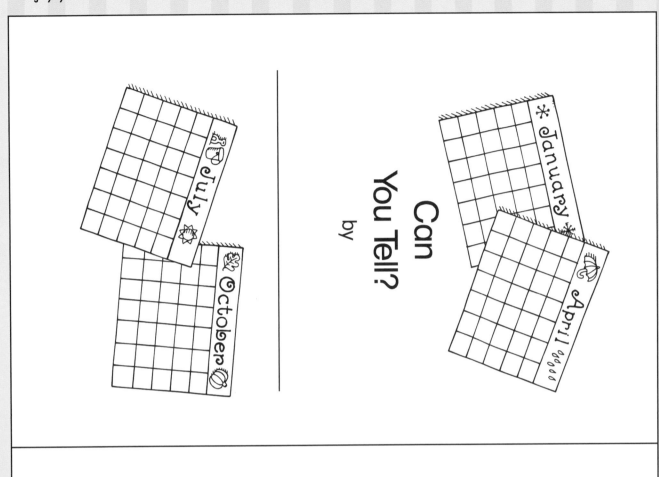

Can
You Tell?

by

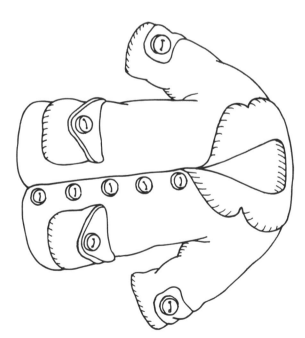

How can you tell it is winter?

I put on my jacket.

1

Dedicated to

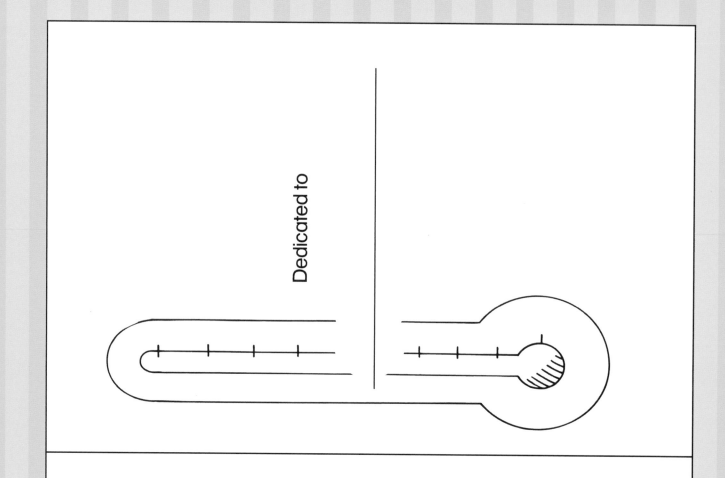

How can you tell it is spring?

I put on my shorts.

2

How can you tell if it is winter,

spring, summer, or fall?

5

How can you tell

it is summer?

I put on my swimsuit.

3

The clothes you put on

tell you all!

The End

6

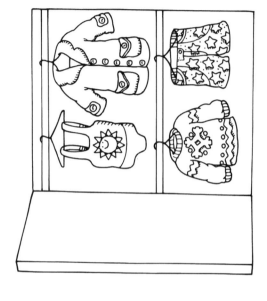

How can you tell it is fall?

I put on my sweater.

4

Little Buddies Phonics Fun • Book 4 • Gr. PreK–K © 2012 Creative Teaching Press

# Answer Key

## PAGE 8

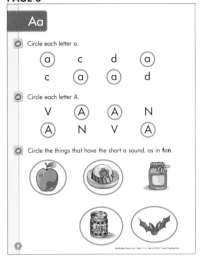

**Aa**

Circle each letter a.

(a)  c  d  (a)
c  (a)  (a)  d

Circle each letter A.

V  (A)  (A)  N
(A)  N  V  (A)

Circle the things that have the short a sound, as in **fan**.

## PAGE 10

map

## PAGE 11

Dan can add hats.

Circle the things that have the sound of short a, as in **fan**.

## PAGE 12

Dan can add cats.

Circle the things that have the sound of short a.

## PAGE 13

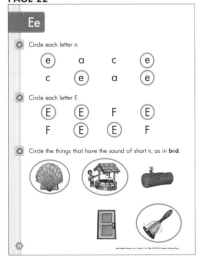

Dan can add bags and tags.

Cross out the things that do not have the sound of short a.

## PAGE 15

Dan can add fans.

Match each picture to its story word.

pants

fans

Dan

## PAGE 16

ants

fans

## PAGE 22

**Ee**

Circle each letter e.

(e)  a  c  (e)
c  (e)  a  (e)

Circle each letter E.

(E)  (E)  F  (E)
F  (E)  (E)  F

Circle the things that have the sound of short e, as in **bed**.

## PAGE 24

tent

## PAGE 25

They set up a tent.

Circle the things that have the sound of short e, as in **bed**.

## PAGE 26

Rex and Tex went to rest in the tent.

Cross out the things that do not have the sound of short e.

## PAGE 27

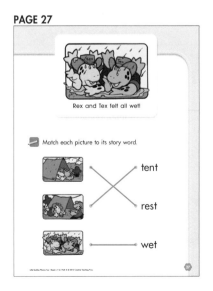

Rex and Tex felt all wet!

Match each picture to its story word.

tent

rest

wet

**PAGE 29**

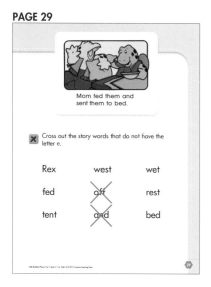

Mom fed them and sent them to bed.

Cross out the story words that do not have the letter e.

Rex     west     wet

fed     ~~off~~     rest

tent     ~~and~~     bed

**PAGE 30**

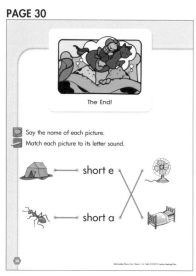

The End!

Say the name of each picture.
Match each picture to its letter sound.

short e

short a

**PAGE 36**

**Ii**

Circle each letter i.

(i)    j    (i)    j
l    j    l    (i)

Circle each letter I.

T    (I)    L    (I)
(I)    L    J    (I)

Circle the things that have the sound of short i, as in hill.

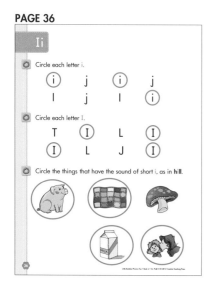

**PAGE 39**

Who will kick it in the net?

Circle the things that have the sound of short i, as in hill.

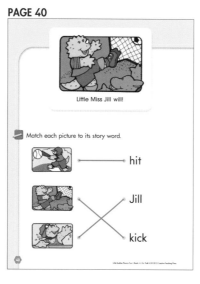

**PAGE 40**

Little Miss Jill will!

Match each picture to its story word.

hit

Jill

kick

**PAGE 41**

Who will swim and win the race?

Cross out the things that do not have the sound of short i.

**PAGE 42**

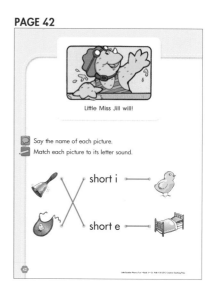

Little Miss Jill will!

Say the name of each picture.
Match each picture to its letter sound.

short i

short e

**PAGE 43**

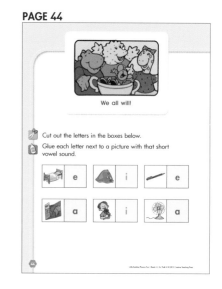

Who will win this?

Cross out the words that do not have the letter i.

Miss     will     Jill

swim     ~~who~~     in

~~ball~~     ~~net~~     ~~team~~

**PAGE 44**

We all will!

Cut out the letters in the boxes below.
Glue each letter next to a picture with that short vowel sound.

e     i     e

a     i     a

**PAGE 38**
ship

## PAGE 50

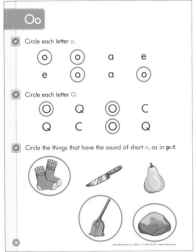

**Oo**

Circle each letter o.

o  o  a  e
e  o  a  o

Circle each letter O.

O  Q  O  C
Q  C  O  Q

Circle the things that have the sound of short o, as in p**o**t.

## PAGE 52
lock

## PAGE 53

Dot's spot is a dog.

Circle the things that have the sound of short o, as in p**o**t.

## PAGE 54

Dot's spot is a frog.

Cross out the things that do not have the sound of short o.

## PAGE 56

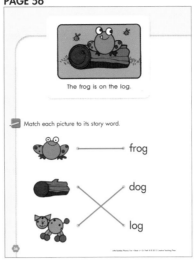

The frog is on the log.

Match each picture to its story word.

frog

dog

log

## PAGE 57

Dot's spot is hot!

Cross out the words that do not have the letter o.

dog      spot     hop
~~can~~   ~~draws~~  hot
frog     lots     ~~she~~

## PAGE 58
hop
hat

## PAGE 64

**u**

Circle each letter u.

a  u  n  u
u  o  n  u

Circle each letter U.

U  A  J  U
N  U  O  J

Circle the things that have the sound of short u, as in cup.

## PAGE 66
rug

## PAGE 67

Jump in the mud
with a thud, thud, thud!

Circle the things that have the sound of short u,
as in **cup**.

## PAGE 68

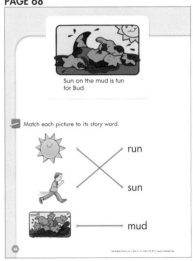

Sun on the mud is fun
for Bud.

Match each picture to its story word.

run

sun

mud

## PAGE 69

Go up to the tub with the
mud on Bud.

Cross out the things that do not have the sound of
short u.

### PAGE 70

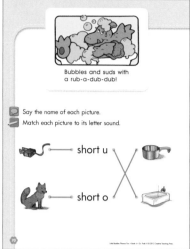

Bubbles and suds with
a rub-a-dub-dub!

Say the name of each picture.

Match each picture to its letter sound.

short u

short o

### PAGE 71

glug glug glug

All clean now, so pull the plug.

Circle the words that have the letter u.

mud    thud    now

fun    with    jump

glug    into    run

### PAGE 72
tub
plug

### PAGE 78

Aa, Ee, Ii
Oo, Uu

Match the letters
a, e, i, o, and u.

a        o
e        u
i        a
o        e
u        i

Match the letters
A, E, I, O, and U.

U        E
E        O
I        A
O        U
A        I

### PAGE 79
Circle van, socks, pants, and lock

### PAGE 80

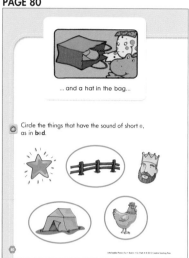

... and a hat in the bag...

Circle the things that have the sound of short e,
as in bed.

### PAGE 81
pin

### PAGE 82

... and pants on the cat.

Circle the things that have the sound of short u,
as in cup.

### PAGE 83

The cat in the hat
spots a rat!

Match the pictures that have the short a and
short o sounds.

### PAGE 84

The cat runs after the rat.

Match the pictures that have short o and short u sounds.

### PAGE 85

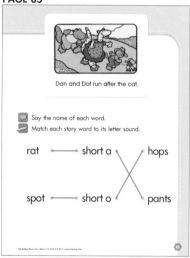

Dan and Dot run after the cat.

Say the name of each word.

Match each story word to its letter sound.

rat        short a        hops

spot        short o        pants

### PAGE 86

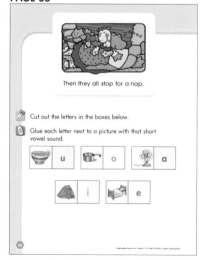

Then they all stop for a nap.

Cut out the letters in the boxes below.

Glue each letter next to a picture with that short
vowel sound.

u    o    a

i    e

# FUNtastic Job!

## Book 4: Short Aa Ee Ii Oo Uu

Signed _____

Name _____

Date _____